My Collection of Report-Story Articles - 'Business' (Part 1)

Entrepreneurship 101

Contents

1. Introduction

As much as businesses are opening up, there are businesses that have failed and or are closing, and all this would involve some degree of 'Entrepreneurship'. Entrepreneurship is a dressed-up word for business, with staff, management, owners and stakeholders, and the ins and outs of business. The following issues to do with Entrepreneurship and business will be analysed in this report.

2. Subjects/Themes

Small-to-medium businesses opening up

Local suburbs, outside of the main suburbs around Australia and the world, are becoming home to more small-to-medium businesses opening up, in addition to existing larger companies.

Teaching people overseas about Entrepreneurism and related things

The Federal Australian Government teaches people overseas in second-world and third-world and war-torn and conflicting countries about business and entrepreneurism to learn to survive, make their own money and not rely too much on a pension. This, as Charles Pickering states, from television show, The Weekly, on a Wednesday evening, helps to reduce the amount of foreign aid and assistance to such nations from better equipped countries like Australia. Similar services are educating people globally on using their own skills and talents or learning some new and or related skill and talent such as in health and fitness, art, culture, technical, professional and so on. This would also help people who are struggling to think properly before delving into dangerous, deceptive, misleading or illegal behaviour to earn money, for example crime.

Real Estate boom feeding business

The real estate boom at the moment in Sydney and Australia, with more town houses, high rise apartments and people making their own mansion-style residence is feeding local businesses, small-to-large, and even calling on a need for more businesses to support this boom. High rise apartments in particular are coming up quite quickly in local areas and local infrastructure will have to support this increase in residents to certain areas.

Local suburbs and mainstream shopping centres like Westfields have businesses that come and go, with an old and faded out saying to support it, 'businesses come and go', just like anything else comes and goes. A solid brand name may not be enough to get by. But what are the things that exist to help these businesses stay afloat.

Strategies and struggles for some businesses

Local Councils have dropped the rent for some small business owners in the local suburbs to provide some assistance. One coffee shop in Sydney's South-West was paying at the time, $60 a week for rent, which sounds too good to be true but it probably had to be done (Personal Experiences – Coffee Shop).

Retail, which is usually in the public eye, would have to have a sale the majority of time with big percentages taken off the regular retail price. Clothing stores are a perfect example of this with department stores like Big W and Rivers. For most of these clothing stores, with sales sometimes as low as some dollars, I would say a sale here and there really would not be enough to pay the expenses and even make a profit (Personal Experiences – Retail Clothing). Although businesses, namely small businesses, have to look after themselves, these small businesses also need to look after their staff and customers. A proper balance must be achieved.

Some small businesses are affected by struggling to pay wages and salary of staff let alone paying themselves and surviving in general. Centrelink, who provides welfare payments to Australians in need, offers income support to certain businesses who are finding it hard to pay an employee properly (Personal Experiences – Office store/Centrelink Payments and Services). The owner of a car dealership in South-West Sydney had to borrow over $300,000 to pay the rent for his yard, pay his staff and as he put it, 'put food on the table'. He eventually went under after 10-12 years in what was once a successful self-owned business (Personal Experiences – Car dealership).

Food and drink and Household items as a form of business

A very common form of business for people is food and drink with coffee and snack eateries like The Coffee Club and Gloria Jeans and mixed business convenience stores here and there. Non-durable items are the way to go for business as people purchase these items all the time, as opposed to durable items like clothing, electrical goods or white goods.

Having a business on the side

Having one's own business is actually another good form of investment, like shares and property for instance. The main activity of this business can be something the person/s is skilled in or likes or enjoys, for example catering and cooking for some mothers and daughters who are often used to cooking meals for family and friends. The business can be on the side, or full-time or part-time. The business owner can be a sole trader, in a partnership or have employees under them, whatever the business owner chooses, needs to or wants to do or what their situation dictates. As shown earlier, some business owners struggle to pay staff as well as pay themselves, so they choose to be a sole-trader for instance.

Business Courses

Whether a person owns and runs a business or not, or works for someone, they may want to further their skills and knowledge about business and Entrepreneurship through the many business courses around, for example, TAFE and Universities, private colleges, private colleges and community colleges. Sometimes 3-4 year or long courses are not the way to go for working and or busy people; hence there are numerous short courses around to help people, employees are or business owners.

An example is the Workers Education Association (WEA) in Sydney which runs a 'Starting a Business' short course for people wanting to commence a business or those wanting to learn about business and entrepreneurship specifically or generally. According to Paul Hanna and his personal development book, 'You Can Do It', a man worked for 20-odd years as a truck driver for Coca-Cola in Australia and did 16 years of short courses at night school in the meantime. He got a managerial job for a position looking after the Asia-Pacific, beating numerous tertiary educated graduates and other multi-levelled managers.

Other areas of business and entrepreneurship education

There are also the business sections of smaller and mainstream newspapers for information on business and entrepreneurship, like the Sydney Morning Herald's 'Small Business' section, providing good practical data with some theory here-and-there. Then of course there is the Internet, which has been a God-send for educating people about various numerous topics, including business and entrepreneurship.

Working for free for work experience

However, sometimes the best skills and knowledge, is experience, on-the-job experience, and volunteering, or accepting lower pay, is a true sign of gaining golden work experience and to show one is in it for the job, not just the money. Some people today refuse to work in a position for a business or company unless the pay, wages or salary, are right. This can be a bad move, especially due to the fact it can lead to lack of job fulfilment and low self-esteem and happiness and contentment.

Ross Gittins, the Business and Economics Editor of the Sydney Morning Herald, was on welfare in Australia for a while, but keeping productive, building on and furthering his skills in writing, before going for and being given a position with Fairfax (Wikipedia, 'Ross Gittins'/Ross Gittins, Sydney Morning Herald, Business). Sometimes a course, although beneficial to an extent, is not always the answer. Some practical job or career experience can do wonders, for example, being a volunteer for a while or accepting a lower paid job to gain that golden job or career experience. Australian Golfer and golfing legend, Greg Norman, would constantly refer to his poem, 'Man in the Mirror', when the media were attacking him he was under-performing, knowing within himself how he was going and what his goals were (Hanna, P. 1997).

Earning and learning about Entrepreneurship

It is one thing to teach about business and related areas and it is another thing to teach about 'Entrepreneurship'. One can be born with a business mind and be a genius in business and entrepreneurship, or one can earn their knowledge, skills, perception and intuition and experience in business. One can be theoretical, whilst another person can be more practical, for example, a TAFE and university course compared to a short course or teaching about business and entrepreneurship and actually doing it and having and owning or working in a business or company. Apart from a few exceptions, i.e. millionaires and billionaires, like Bill Gates of Microsoft and Richard Branson of Virgin, people are usually a mix of both being business-minded and entrepreneurial and practicing business, theoretical and practical, although there are some extremes there. There are numerous ways, as discussed already, people can improve and develop their business and entrepreneurial development.

Personal Development in business

A combination of education and courses, work experience, networking and personal perception and intuition come together to bring about an entrepreneur's personal development. Some go into business during or after education, and continue, sometimes blindly and being unaware or reluctant to pursue further education, skills and experience. Some feel fine where they are in business as entrepreneurs and will or will not justify improving and developing themselves in some way. Remember the example previously about how a Coca-Cola truck driver undertook 16 years of night school. It does not have to be 16 years and can just be the odd course from time-to-time, or volunteer work experience at the company or area or project you always wanted to work at. You might even do one course all your life and that could be enough. As the saying goes, 'something is better than nothing'. Some do more, as in 16 years of night school, and some do less, as one course their whole life; as long as the worker makes sure they pick up, remember and learn something along the way, and make it work successfully in the business they are, that is what counts.

Networking as a business investment

Networking, whether as a social tool and or business investment, is a fantastic medium to improve one's knowledge, skills and experience of business and entrepreneurship. Examples of Networking are groups linked to industry associations and actual businesses and companies and business investment firms like Network 21-Amway, Isagenix and GNLD and USANA. These companies follow trends like finance, health and household goods, using consumerism of purchasing goods and word-of-mouth, to provide people the experience and money on the latest business and information lines. Networking businesses teach people first-hand knowledge on how to deal with people and customers (people skills), how to run a business like an investment, how to earn and manage money, goal-setting and planning and helping others and charity. It is a perfect way to condition one's entrepreneurship.

Entrepreneurship in other countries

Australia might be afraid of becoming like other countries like America, India and China where 'Entrepreneurship' has allowed business ideas and practice to just flow, in Australian terms, too freely, with numerous millionaires and billionaires. The media has shown Australia's own millionaires and billionaires, such as James Packer and Rupert Murdoch, Henry Tinkler and Gina Rinehart, and either their rise or fall. Some have been shown to have fallen of lately, losing large amounts of money and even going bankrupt. Then again, the media tends to explore the negative angle on things and this might not be the case for other wealthy business people in Australia. This form of entrepreneurship teaches principles of Capitalism and greed and selfishness and not of charity, generosity and good moral values.

Good moral values in business

Australia for example is largely a Christian country which has not let big money enter its borders. The majority of people have spiritual and religious values as to not be corrupted by money. For example, there is sport in Australia, despite some changes, has not given out to large sums of money like in sports in North America and Europe. There is also a big gap between rich and poor in these nations, as well as some developed and third-world countries, with Australia, acknowledging the people with money and who are comfortable or well-off, look after its people through the welfare system titled Centrelink. Centrelink in Australia even offers courses on business for people looking to get off welfare or make some extra money whilst on welfare.

Teaching people about entrepreneurship to support economy

Entrepreneurship, on a positive note, can also be a way to educate people in Australia and globally to support their economy. A person may not exactly want to buy something, but if it means supporting a business owned by someone they know or have befriended, and in turn supporting the local or wider economy, then they would do it. The current Tony Abbott-Joe Hockey Liberal Party Australian Government have come out with a harsh and tough budget that supports growing the economy. This budget, with Liberals being more business-minded in general compared to Labor, in particular is a quick way to generate money for the economy when really, without walking in a straight line and keeping some drama, other measures could have been taken to make some money for the economy instead of targeting Labor's vulnerable areas of health, education and welfare.

Entrepreneurship issues

Multi-Skilling

People in business in today's working environment should, and sometimes need to be proficient in more than one area of expertise. The requirement to need and do more in businesses in general is prevalent these days than ever before. Small-to-medium businesses already have staff do a number of tasks and duties. In fact, such businesses provide a perfect environment for multi-skilling to thrive, for example, being expert in sales and marketing or accounting and then also cleaning and maintaining the store as something else that needs to be carried out. Some staff in bigger companies have actually started out and learned multi-skilling principles and action from small-to-medium businesses and can fit into almost any working environment because of this. Some examples of multi-skilling have been combining roles of driver and conductor (fares) at State Transit government buses in Sydney and retail stores globally.

Day-to-day running of business

Like multi-skilling, entrepreneurs need to manage, if not juggle, the everyday functioning of their business. Larger companies would not necessarily allow this as each worker is sectioned-off to a certain area, whereas small-to-medium businesses give a staffer the opportunity to be into everything. A staffer in this environment would surely feel the difference, sooner or later, at a bigger company by not being able to breathe and do other tasks and duties. It is amazing how it is the smaller day-to-day tasks and duties that can be quite an effort and need to be done, such as budgeting (for example, counting the till), cleaning, display of store or business and securing the premises. Taking the display of a store for instance, a busy day of shopping can leave the store in a mess with products or display items left everywhere with no time to correct the problem, even with mistakes in the till.

Entrepreneurship and Politics

Surely the Australian and local Governments can better invest in the countries' businesses, and the people who work for them. We Australians have to work for these businesses, like these businesses and their owners need to survive and make ends meet for themselves and their families as well.

Perhaps the Labor and Liberal parties need to get back to, or alter, their foundational beliefs and values. Although it is fairly obvious, with titles of Labor and Liberal, some may not see it that way with each of these two major parties acting like the other (Australian Labor Party web-site, www.alp.org.au/ Liberal Party of Australia, www.liberal.org.au).

Labor can stand for businesses as well as the workers, customers and other stakeholders, and a good work ethic in all facets of life. Looking at this, it is obvious why Labor is, and still is in power today with a power-to-all emphasis. Liberal however leads to multi-definitions. Liberal can stand for a free, democratic country and ideals, which does sounds good, but then being free and happy can lead to being too free and happy and in turn stereotypes like hippies, nudist beaches, car hoons and drug takers. But Liberal can also stand for free and healthy businesses on a whole, not just the general population, i.e. the workers, customers and other stakeholders in a business.

Although the Howard Government (Liberals) stood firm with Australia in general for quite some years, so has Labor, and of course this needs to be vigilantly maintained. Both parties have not allowed too much into our shores, maintaining our way of life here, although the lessening of Union power, and the 'WorkChoice' initiative, was a poor choice as it took some of the workers' powers away (Liberal Party of Australia).

Then there are those people who are on welfare, and the 'Work for the Dole' system. Kevin Rudd of Labor got rid of this system when he was in power, but there have been talks of bringing it back in. Businesses can benefit from this labour and people on welfare can gain some new skills and experience, for example volunteering or work experience. It is also these businesses, as well as other high-earning people in Australia, who pay for these peoples' welfare payments (Australian Labor Party).

However, there are many legitimate cases of people living on welfare. Times are tougher compared to our parents' and grandparents' years and people have received payments because they have become sick or ill, disabled or other life commitments like a starting a family. There have been some sad and sorry souls who got sick, having to go on welfare, and even later died, because of stresses of modern working and life in general. So it is best to tread carefully with this area (Australian Labor Party).

3. Conclusion

So what we will have from this entrepreneurialism? In general, there could be healthy, flourishing businesses, giving staff a great job or career, solid pay and good working conditions. But then again, the risk with entrepreneurialism is having more high-flying and reckless millionaires and billionaires floating around Australia. So some assistance and controls need to be there and Australia is good for that (SME World, March 2009/Centrelink Payments and Services).

4. Bibliography

- Australian Government, Centrelink Payments and Services
- Australian Labor Party, www.alp.org.au
- Australian Society of Entrepreneurs (2 July, 2012) 'Small Business Failure Rates, What's the Reasons'
- Hanna, Paul. (1997) 'You Can Do It' (Personal Development book)
- Liberal Party of Australia, www.liberal.org.au
- Personal experiences: - South-West Sydney (Coffee Shop, Retail – Clothing, Office store, Car dealership)
  - Own Self-Employed Business
- Ross Gittins, Sydney Morning Herald, Business
- SME World (Small Entrepreneurs) (March 2009) 'America Leads in Entrepreneurialism'
- Sydney Morning Herald, 'Small Business' section
- Wikipedia, 'Ross Gittins'

Nothing Bouris about Mark Bouris:

A take on Australian businessman Mark Bouris

Contents

1. Subjects/Themes
- His business acumen
- Public man with a Private Life
- Getting the best out of the people in his businesses
- Wizard Home Loans
→ <u>Wizard and Banks</u>

- Mark Bouris and Kerry and James Packer
- Bouris and Yellow Brick Road and Celebrity Apprentice
- Bouris and the Sydney City/Easts Rugby League team
- Selling Wizard to General Electric Corporation
- Bouris' property sale
- Bouris' immediate family
- Bouris' Partners and Children

2. Bibliography

1. Subjects/Themes

His business acumen

Bouris is not ruthless as he has regards for other people. Bouris is very hard working, tough-minded, competitive, disciplined, creative, has a strong work ethic and is a natural born leader with fantastic people skills, wanting to be the best at what he does. James Packer described Bouris as being "street smart with serious intelligence...he looks at complex issues and works his way through them with a great deal of sophistication." Bouris has quite a few extracurricular activities like love of beautiful cars, art and real estate like a farm in Byron Bay.

Mark Bouris has got the goods as a slick, professional and smart businessman. His strategies and action plans have put him at the forefront of business and finance in Australia.

He has a Bachelors and Masters in Commerce. Bouris worked as a Chartered Accountant in the initial stages of his career and then in a law firm for about seven years. He made mistakes with some investments when he was younger but learned from them. This shows no one is perfect and Bouris should have been allowed to make mistakes. Bouris was into money and business, with the incentives and indulgences that went along with it.

Public man with a Private Life

Behind the public image lies a very private man. Bouris has different personas, one for work and the other for home and family life. He does not mess around and is straightforward, telling people what he thinks. He's not good at sympathy and when a person gets upset.

Bouris is a bit undisciplined at home, being more relaxed. His kids are a great grounding force, with sometimes his public persona getting somewhat carried away. Martha, Bouris' second wife, states how she would like Bouris to broaden his social life, being somewhat of private man.

Getting the best out of the people in his businesses

His number one goal is getting the best possible outcome from the people in his organization. He drives each one of his people, even giving them a hug when need be.

Wizard Home Loans

Bouris actually found the word Wizard from the dictionary, making a list of 20 names to select from. In time, Wizard became one of the best mortgage companies in Australia. A lot of people have done well through Wizard with Bouris helping them to build their wealth.

Bouris' millions have not come overnight, they have taken time. His Wizard Home Loans sponsored the NSW Blues State of Origin team when the great half Andrew Johns was playing for the team. Just think of the level of skill and expertise it would have taken to get Wizard Home Loans to sponsor a successful outfit as the NSW Blues State of Origin team.

Wizard and Banks

Wizard took advantage of a weakness and void and deregulation of the mortgage industry from the mainstream banks, going after a piece of the market. Mark looks to provide a certain reputation and image to Wizard. Symonds and Bouris were pioneers in the industry. According to Adrian Bouris, Mark's brother, "Banks, at the time, were alienating their customers, introducing fees, having long queues and not passing on interest savings... and Wizard took advantage of that." Again Adrian Bouris states how, "Wizard's success relied upon being in the right place at the right time, being innovative and the culture of the people." Bouris thoroughly took advantage of any threat that came his or Wizard's way.

Wizard, along with the also popular Aussie Home Loans of John Symonds, brought in more affordable products and better loans. The difference with Aussie and Wizard was that Wizard brought in branches and Aussie was not into that at the time.

There are around 250 branches of Wizard in Australia and New Zealand, similar to the distribution of McDonald's – "At Wizard, the person who runs the branch, owns the branch. It is purely commission with no wage. But there is definitely an incentive there to earn money...some of the branches earn around a million a year."

Mark Bouris and Kerry and James Packer

Bouris struck a deal with Packer. Kerry Packer initially wanted someone in Bouris who had been there done that, and had worked for and lost money and learned their lesson from it. Packer was an in-depth thinker who was one step ahead, almost like a sage (wise man) in a way. Kerry liked Mark; both respected one another and had a good friendship.

The Packers put a lot of money into Bouris' Wizard and the Packers made five times their money. Channel 9 and ACP Properties, part owned by the Packers, were of great benefit to Wizard at the time. An example of this was the successful sponsorship of the NSW Blues State of Origin team. As a part of its branding and marketing strategy, Bouris states how millions of dollars went into sponsoring various sports in Australia like Rugby League, AFL and Rugby Union, and also some lifestyle programs on television.

Bouris also appeared in some of the Wizard advertisements and his good looks and charm also added a solid element to the Wizard brand. Adrian Bouris stated how his brother Mark was always a bit of a chick magnet.

Bouris and Yellow Brick Road and Celebrity Apprentice

As if Wizard Home Loans would be enough, now Yellow Brick Road is taking Bouris' finance savvy to a new level. Yellow Brick Road (YBR) is a recent finance business created by Mark Bouris. Bouris' salary from YBR is said to be $750,000 base salary. YBR was made popular by Bouris appearing and taking part in the ever popular TV show Celebrity Apprentice in Australia. On the show, Bouris is the boss and judge of supposed famous apprentices from all walks of life.

Bouris sees Celebrity Apprentice as a perfect way to enhance the focus of YBR's products and services, by having an effective marketing spend across television and digital marketing. Other marketing and advertising services with Channel Nine, under the Packers, came to around $2.5 million over two years. YBR's sponsorship of Celebrity Apprentice came to around $883,000. American Billionaire Donald Trump also acts in the US version of Celebrity Apprentice with the popular line, 'Your Fired', if the apprentice does not perform as expected (Kruger, C. August 3, 2015).

Bouris and the Sydney City/Easts Rugby League team

Bouris got involved with the Sydney City, or Easts Rugby League team. He has been on the board of the team for a few years now. Bouris takes his boys to watch the Roosters at home games. Mark has earned some great friendships whilst being at the Roosters with "Nick Politis, Peter Newton, David Gyngell and of course James Packer." He takes advantage of opportunities that come his way.

Selling Wizard to General Electric Corporation

Bouris made one of the biggest and important decisions of his career by selling Wizard to General Electric Organisation (GEC), or GEC Money, in December 2004, for $400 million. It took over a year to sell. GEC is one of the largest companies in the world, like the oil company Exxon, with revenues of about $165 billion dollars and operating in 51 countries. GE Money is one of six businesses of GEC. Selling to GEC made Wizard competitive with the riches of the banks. GE even sent teams of anonymous people to scour Wizard in every detail.

Bouris remained as Chairman of what is now Wizard International in 2006, after the GE sale. With the sale to GE, Bouris is bringing out other products like insurance products, personal loan products, credit cards and other things that banks usually do. Bouris has pushed and challenged Wizard and GE by helping GE grow its mortgage wing in the countries it operates under, like Europe, Latin America, Asia and India.

Bouris' property sale

Bouris bought into once was Sydney's tallest residential building a decade ago, with a three bedroom apartment to create a five bedroom spread over 420 square metres.

He now has a property in Watson's Bay of a 25-year lease on an 1881-built heritage residence on Camp Cove. Bouris earned more than $8 million for his larger two-storey home. (Macken, L. January 30, 2015)

Bouris' immediate family

Bouris' father came from Greece in the late 1940's and his mother was Irish-Catholic background. Mark came from a good and hardworking family where he became trained for this type of living. Bouris' initial good family upbringing and routine has flowed onto his own family. Bouris' father had a café in the central and famous George Street in the city. He was also a factory worker and at one stage had seven jobs, with one full-time job and six part-time jobs. His mother had a night-time occupation. They were brought up in the rough-and-tough Punchbowl in the Canterbury-Bankstown area of Western Sydney, known to be a Rugby League-strong region. Mark's mother Marsha also believed in hard work and for working for what you want in life without it being given to you.

Bouris is the oldest sibling in the family and has three younger brothers who play an important part in his life. Bouris is very caring, but strict and livable with his family. He does swimming, weight training and self-defence with his family. Their father was good with his hands and passed this onto the Bouris boys.

Mark's brother Dane got into property development and management and investment, not taking a liking to working at Mark's Wizard at first. This family business taught Dane to be ambitious and have that hunger for success and the better things in life. Mark's brother Adrian on the other hand has been with Wizard all his life. Mark's father George said it was good to see all his family work together and relying on each other.

Bouris' Partners and Children

Bouris has aimed to provide a happy, stabilized and well-educated family. He has been married twice. He has one child to the first marriage and three children to the second marriage. He acknowledged how marriage ending is a complex thing. It would also be hard to be single whilst in the public eye, as well as look after such relationships. He has been single for 18 months. His success at business interests and level of support to give to his kids also influenced the relationship with his partners. He currently has good relationships with his children and good friendships with his former partners, and he looks to maintain these great relationships and friendships.

When Mark's second wife had been chronically ill, he spent more time with his children – "Unless I have a pressing engagement for work, I would spend every night of the week with the children at home, having a meal with them."

2. Bibliography

- ABC (August 14, 2006) 'Making a Mark', <u>Australian Story</u>
- Kruger, Colin (August 3, 2015) 'Nine's Celebrity Apprentices won't stray from Mark Bouris' Yellow Brick Road', <u>Sydney Morning Herald</u>
- Macken, Lucy. (January 30, 2015) 'Title Deeds: Mark Bouris sells city pad for more than $8 million', <u>Domain</u>

Penalty Rates and related issues:

Penalty Rates, Abbott Government and Australia

Contents

1. **Subjects/Themes**
   - **Productivity Commission Report**
   - **Problems found with Fair Work Commission**
   - **Lessons learned from 'WorkChoices'**
   - **Importance of Weekends**
   - **Small Businesses**
   - **Negotiate Wage/Salary Level**
   - **Other initiatives or incentives from business to employee**
   - **Consumers to benefit from Penalty Rates**
   - **Hospitality, Retail and Distributive sector hit**
   - **Rural Communities**
   - **Support from Government**
   - **Moral, Spiritual and Religious significance**
2. **Conclusion**
3. Bibliography

1. Subjects/Themes

Productivity Commission Report

The independent government Productivity Commission has constructed a report for the Abbott government into workplace relations detailing a wide range of potential changes, including penalty rates. The government wants to 'turn Sunday penalty rates into Saturday penalty rates'. It is an overview of modern awards that brought a reduction to casual penalty rates. Under such proposed changes, "employees would be able to take public holidays at a different time with full penalty rates and negotiate longer annual leave [20 day] with likely pay rises. (Lee, J. Kenny, M. August 4, 2015)" The changes were about fixing weaknesses not disrupting long-term rights and protections of employees. An example is keeping the minimum wage and award the same for employees. However, Australian Council of Trade Unions (ACTU) secretary believes the opposite and that the proposed changes "are an attack on penalty rates, rights at work and the minimum wage. (Riga, R. August 6, 2015)."

It is about gaining a national approach, with the unions and Labour involved, carefully considering all recommendations and taking it to the battleground of the 2016 election where the Australian people will either endorse the changes or not (Lee, J. and Kenny, M. August 4, 2015).

The draft report, and the Fair Work Commission's modernization standards, found there were few problems with the current system and that generally the system was working well. Under the report, there were few wage problems, inflation low and unemployment shorter with more casual work on offer. (Lee, J. Kenny, M. August 4, 2015).

Problems found with Fair Work Commission

The report by the Productivity Commission found flaws with the structures of the Fair Work Commission. There were biases against some commissioners, inconsistencies between members' decisions, lacking rigour in its labour market analysis, poorly equipped as a tribunal, overly legalistic, employers ill-treated and forced to pay compensation against misbehaving employees and employers exploiting migrant workers. It seems to be going back and forth between employer and employee and the middle men. There is a lot there, so this puts into question the actual fairness of the Fair Work Commission. Commissioners selected from the union movement, on the contrary, which Labour works with, would act more appropriately than the Fair Work Commission by upholding things like unfair dismissal. (Lee, J. Kenny, M. August 4, 2015)

Lessons learned from 'WorkChoices'

Although Coalition has seemingly learned its lessons from the Howard government's WorkChoices policy, problems are arising with a divide in the workforce issue – "Australians spoke loud and clear in 2007 [against WorkChoices]. We [Liberals] learned that lesson immediately after the election." (Lee, J, and Kenny, M. August 4, 2015). Shadow Employment Minister, Brendan O'Connor, states how the problem is with the enterprise contracts where some people are doing the same job but getting unequal pay and standards. O'Connor said the "penalty rate cuts were 'unfair'". Australian Council of Trade Unions secretary, Dave Oliver, said the commission's report was like "a Trojan horse that's going to deliver WorkChoices part two," with some elements worse than the original WorkChoices (Lee, J. and Kenny, M. August 4, 2015) This stance contradicts the Productivity Commission's findings that there were few flaws from the current workplace system.

Importance of Weekends

Australian Prime Minister, Tony Abbott stated how weekends were not being used properly with entire cities and towns being shut down – "…complaining entire towns are being shut down on Sundays. (Owens, J. August 6, 2015)" There are people who love to work and would even work weekends, either the Saturday and or Sunday. Lee and Kenny state how weekend services are more in demand over the past few decades, with more women working, lower levels of church goers and longer shopping hours, for example a Thursday evening. The money these people earn on weekends goes to helping themselves and raising their families. Ms Eurling works 4am to 12pm midday, five days a week, including on Saturdays and Sundays. She works at Sydney Casiono, and to her credit, has been at the Casino 20 years. Ms Eurling states how she "does the shifts for the children and the penalty rates are very important to us." (Patty, A. August 8, 2015).

There is more money to be earned on weekends, but it can sometimes come at a cost. Alternatively, those who work on weekends do not get to see their family as often – "Saturdays and Sundays are also important time with the family, and she misses seeing the children's weekend sport." Company Deloitte Access Economics did a study about the notion that "Sunday is still considered a special day of significance." With this study, it was "found that 55 per cent of respondents said Saturday and Sunday were equally important. Only 31 per cent said Sunday was more significant. (Patty, A. August 8, 2015)." Then there are those who are Monday to Friday staff and have the weekends free to do some activity, like shopping and people and businesses helping one another, hence an economy and where weekend businesses come in. As the saying goes, 'someone has got to do it [weekend work].'

Small Businesses

Some small businesses are not like larger businesses and understand properly about workplace relations and employment contracts, or as stated, 'enterprise contacts'. Small businesses found these enterprise contracts confronting and complex, having to negotiate themselves about award rates, with the problem of having to educate themselves and staff about the enterprise contracts. (Lee, J. Kenny, M. August 4, 2015) Riga states how it is easier for multinationals and corporates, but you have to come "back to the engine room of the economy, the small-to-medium sized businesses... It [penalty rates] has got to be made simpler and more effective for these smaller businesses." (Riga, R. August 6, 2015).

However, from a business point of view, a cut in penalty rates has employment and economic benefits to small-to-medium sized businesses by generating more profits and employing more people – "it's not a case of this evil employer trying to rip off the worker, it is a case of businesses struggling to survive and the more they can employ and hence grow and develop."(Riga, R. August 6, 2015). Research by Deloitte Access Economics goes against these benefits of cutting penalty rates by stating it would "depress labour demand, push up consumer prices and embody an outmoded view of weekends being special. (Owens, J. August 6, 2015).

But the rent these businesses pay would surely stretch the whole week, 7 days a week, according to local Council rules and regulations. Employers could get employees working on a voluntary basis or low wage/salary to work on the weekend because the rent is paid until then. The question is what businesses are doing on the weekend since they have already paid the rent. If the rent is paid for the week, it would be a waste to not stay open. Then the next is does the employer work themselves or use employees to do some or all of the work for them, hence penalty rates. Business is business; there would be someone who would want to work on the weekend, and perhaps the employer can take a break often or now and again.

Negotiate Wage/Salary Level

A wage/salary level, or minimum wage, should be negotiated in this time between between Liberals and Labour and their delegates and representatives. There are some who need the weekend money and those who do not mind earning extra money from employers. Therefore a wage/salary level should be redrawn according to each person's circumstances. It is the lower paid of the workforce who could probably suffer the most. Shadow Employment Minister, Brendan O'Connor, states "If you cut the take-home pay for the lowest paid, most vulnerable, second-class citizens and young people in this country, about four million, you starve the economy because they spend all of their savings…and give it over to employers" (Lee, J. Kenny, M. August 4, 2015)

Other initiatives or incentives from business to employee

While employees might lose out on penalty rates cuts, they may gain in other ways. Perhaps the businesses involved, as well as government could find others means and incentives to look after and support the employee other than money. Examples of this are food and drink, coupons, gift vouchers, rewards, incentives, initiatives, ideas and projects.

Consumers to benefit from Penalty Rates

Deregulated penalty rates will mean consumers will greatly benefit from them by more convenience and lower prices (Lee, J. Kenny, M, August 4, 2015). Businesses can take the money normally used for penalty rates and put it back into the business for consumers to enjoy.

Hospitality, Retail and Distributive sector hit

A cut to penalty rates would greatly affect service sectors like hospitality, retail, cleaning and distributive, who rely heavily on penalty rates. A restauranter in Geelong, Victoria, Maria Versace, relies on penalty rates to help raise her family, like Ms. Eurling from Sydney Casino. The national secretary of the Shop, Distributive and Allied Employee's Association, which hospitality, retail and distribution come under, states "the retail and hospitality sectors would be hardest hit." Australian Chamber of Commerce and Industry Chief Executive, Kate Carnell, highlighted how "the retail sector has changed fundamentally over the last 20 years in terms of Sunday openings. (Patty, A. August 8, 2015).

Rural Communities

Rural people would be one of the hardest hit by a strike to weekend penalty rates. A lot of people living in rural areas rely on weekend penalty rates. More people are usually situated in and are attracted to city areas where all the people and action is, compared to regional/rural areas where it is a bit quieter. Patty highlights the effect of penalty rates to rural/regional areas.

Patty states, "Any move to scrap penalty rates would have a disproportionate impact on our rural communities." (Patty, A. August 8, 2015). Patty goes on to state how the McKell Institute found that "regional [rural] Australia would collectively lose between $370 million to $691 million a year if penalty rates were cut...disposable income in regional areas would reduce by up to $748.3 million a year. (Patty, A. August 8, 2015)" National President of union United Voice, Jo-Anne Scholfied, highlights the deeper and growing rift between city and country areas and the haves and have-nots (Patty, A. August 8, 2015). After all this time, and all that has been achieved, still remains the gap between rich and poor, including penalty rates.

Support from Government

To deal with this penalty rates issue, small-to-medium-sized businesses would need some assistance from Government, as would larger businesses and corporations. This is especially for people who would suffer the loss of their income from penalty rates on weekends. Money lost from a weekend can be reimbursed from other means, for example a bonus, incentive or tax refund.

Moral, Spiritual and Religious significance

For some people, working all week, and keeping weekends free is important to them. They have time to relax, see family and friends, do a sport or recreation, do a hobby or interest and practice their moral, spiritual and religious faith. In Christianity, the Sunday is the Holy Sabbath, the day of rest to give to God and religion and immediate and important people in one's life. Lee and Kenny highlight how weekend work has grown in demand as there are fewer Church-goers. These people run the risk of getting too worldly and societal and risk going down the wrong track. (August 4, 2015).

2. Conclusion

The Productivity Commission states there only a few flaws in the current system. Labour and union movement state otherwise, calling the draft report an attack on penalty rates and the like. One could go either way, but then again one thing can lead to the rest. If penalty rates are minimized, altered or eradicated, the Abbott government states the employees and employers will be reimbursed in some way or another. It could be worth a try but closely monitored by Liberal, Labour and Senate. Either way, something good would surely come from this, especially after the uproar over the Howard government's WorkChoices some years back.

3. Bibliography

- Lee, Jane. Kenny, Mark. (August 4, 2015) 'Sunday penalty rates for hospitality, retail workers could fall to Saturday levels: Productivity Commission report', <u>Sydney Morning Herald</u>

- Owens, Jared. (August 6, 2015) 'Abbott puts pressure over weekend penalty rates', <u>The Australian</u>

- Patty, Anna. (August 8, 2015) 'Workers count the cost to penalty rates of turning Sunday into Saturday', <u>Sydney Morning Herald</u>

- Riga, Rachel. (August 6, 2015) 'Proposal to cut hospitality, retail Sunday penalty rates a plus for small traders says Hervey Bay group', <u>ABC News</u>

Sports Sponsorship the name of the game

Looking at the effectiveness of sports sponsorship

Australia is a sporting nation and we love our sport. We are also in the middle of a health and fitness boom, with healthy being the norm. So it would make perfect sense for businesses and organizations to want to be associated with Australia's variety of sports clubs, teams and players. But the sports, teams and players need these businesses and organizations too for income and support. This leads into the area of 'Sports Sponsorship'. The New South Wales Department of Sport Recreation in Australia states how Sports Sponsorship 'helps build reputation and image within the community; increases awareness, participation and buying; generates goodwill and can be considered as a cost-effective alternative to traditional advertising' (NSW Department of Sport and Recreation, 'Sponsorship')

Sports Sponsorship has grown phenomenally in the last 10 years and more, not just in Australia, but globally, to be an important member of the marketing mix. Media exposure is more expensive and sports sponsorship is cost-effective, even free at times. However, from a negative viewpoint, Millward Brown state consumers are not actively looking for brands when they are exposed to it via sports sponsorship (Millward Brown (October 2006)) . It is highly likely for a brand to be missed or ignored, for example by young males. Therefore sports sponsorship needs to be integrated with other media and marketing. Additionally, There is a lower degree of control and uncertainty with sports sponsorship with the sponsored event, team or person and their or others' performance and behavior (Millward Brown (October 2006)) For example, a man with a flare ran onto the court at the 2013 French Open Men's Tennis final, and this has been done before, and punching and urinating in Rugby League.

Jalleh, G. et al state that in Australia in 1996-1997 $466.5 million was spent on sponsorship, of which $281.9 million was channelled into sports, the most out of any area compared to trade and conferences, education and arts and culture. This highlights the significance Australian society places on sport In 2001, businesses globally will spend more than $21.6 billion sponsoring, not just sports, but arts, entertainment, causes and events. How much of the $21.6 billion was actually from Australia is worth finding out (Jalleh et al (Spring 2002)).

As an elite sporting organization, the Australian Sports Commission, like some other businesses has some well thought out and researched sponsors who are directly and indirectly linked to sport, such as the sports drink Gatorade and Nestle brand of sweets and chocolate drinks (Australian Sports Commission, 'Sponsorship'). The Australian Sports Commission, like some other businesses has stringent requirements to make a business it's sponsor and partner. Partner, now that's a word. Partner is more connotative of a more intimate and closer relationship, trusting and assisting one another to reach each other's goals. Account managers of these businesses and organizations, like the Australian Sports Commission, take the time to tailor programs and leverage strategies delivering on business and marketing objectives (Australian Sports Commission, 'Sponsorship').

Sports in general would be looking for like-minded 'partners' committed to such things as excellence, research, innovation, inclusion, performance, leadership, and most importantly, the health and wellbeing of Australians (Australian Sports Commission, 'Sponsorship'). An area which will be looked at later is bringing on sponsors and partners who are not exactly classed as healthy, like the tobacco companies, fast food, alcohol and soft drink. Most of these products are considered vices and or indulgences by many people in society.

An effective way to see if sports sponsorship is working is to look at the consumer behavior, not just the commercial interests, i.e. financial performance. A combined, integrated approach is needed, like sponsorship in the marketing mix. The consumers' interests and obtaining the money must be a joint affair. According to Grohs, R. et al, 'the main goal of sponsorship in general is being more directly associated with consumer behavior by boasting brand awareness and brand attitude and company image' (Grohs, Wagner, and Vsetecka (April 2004)). Target marketing is an important part of this as reaching the correct consumers, not just treating them right, is vital.

Businesses are looking to 'decentralize' (in business jargon) their business functions, including marketing and sponsorship, to take in and listen to the needs, wants and interests of its employees, as well as the consumer. Top management has contact with the lower and ground levels, or a higher spending or loyal consumer and a lower spending or loyal consumer. Keeping the sponsor happy is also paramount for sports, maybe not locally, but definitely for large scale or elite sports. Network Marketing, such as Amway, Isagenix and USANA, which uses word-of-mouth and consumerism of buying products, is a good example of decentralization at work where everyone is on the same level and there is a level playing field to help each other earn money and reach their goals.

Grohs, R. et al states how measurement of consumer behaviour is easy, straightforward and not very costly, but some businesses are reluctant to do it (Grohs, Wagner, and Vsetecka (April 2004)). Examples are quick surveys in the street, over-the-counter, on the telephone and on a business' web-site. In stating this, the only way for sports sponsorship to be effective is to include, prepare and create 'evaluation' into sports sponsorship from the start, not just half-heartedly. A study by Thjomoe et al asked Norwegian firms how they evaluated their sponsorship and its goals with regards to brand awareness and brand attitude and business image. There were 70-80 firms who agreed with sponsoring to increase brand awareness and brand attitude and improve image. Only just above 15% of these firms would study brand perceptions before and after sponsorship, and this can be applied to Australian businesses too (Grohs, Wagner, and Vsetecka (April 2004)). Measuring media coverage and exposure, for example Media Monitors in Australia, is still most widely used by managers in about 70% of sponsorships (Grohs, Wagner, and Vsetecka (April 2004)). Image studies though are mainly kept to large sports sponsorships of say the FIFA World Cup and Olympic Games. A look at smaller businesses and sports sponsorship is a bit later.

One of the predominant reasons for this reluctance of businesses to measure their sponsorships is competition through 'ambush marketing' (Grohs, Wagner, and Vsetecka (April 2004)). This is where consumers believe incorrectly that other companies are the actual sponsors of an event. At the 2008 Beijing Olympics, Pepsi upstaged Coca-Cola's $400 million spent on the Olympics buy running an online competition. A survey at the end of the Olympics had 60% of people in China thinking that Pepsi was the main sponsor. Surely, Pepsi should realize they are disturbing Coca-Cola like this, and this competition, especially during an Olympic Games, would turn to sponsor-to-sponsor fighting, with consumers and the public caught in the middle (Grohs, Wagner, and Vsetecka (April 2004)). During the 1988 Winter Olympics, viewers were asked who they thought were the official sponsors. Eleven of the 20 brands most often identified as worldwide sponsors of the 1988 Winter Olympics were not in fact sponsors (Grohs, Wagner, and Vsetecka (April 2004)).

Taking over from an existing sponsor can be tough, but with eagerness and planning, it can work. The following are two scenarios for and against sponsors taking over from an existing sponsor. Millward Brown state how Brand 2 took over sponsorship of a sports event in 1998, but by 2000, more people still associated the event with the original sponsor. Brand 2 had to work hard to change this position, using PR and creativity (Millward Brown (October 2006)) .. But it was those years between 1998 and 2000 that should have been put to better use by Brand 2, instead of catching up. The other scenario was Bridgestone, who were a bit more prepared than Brand 2 in the first scenario, when electronics firm NEC dropped its sponsorship of the PGA Golf tour. Bridgestone even added to its successful sponsorship of the PGA Golf tour by adding its Bridgestone Golf brand (Millward Brown (October 2006)) .

Going back to health sports sponsorship, Jalleh et al highlights how one thing the not-so- healthy companies did was show how effective sponsorship can be for other companies (Jalleh et al (Spring 2002)). Health and non-Health related businesses are now clamoring to be associated with sports. McDonald's, close to Australia's most well known fast food chain, is associated with sports on a big level and local level. With alcohol sponsorship, Bundaberg Rum is with the Australian Wallabies (Rugby Union), Four X with the Queensland Maroons NRL State team and Bud Light with Ultimate Fighting Championship (UFC). Then there is the international gambling web-site, Bet365, being associated with most sports around the world, and of course gambling is another taboo and vice.

Millward Brown states how all these sports, including other adventurous and extreme sports, have young males as their primary target market that other media might find difficult to reach (Millward Brown (October 2006)) . Health is somewhat of a factor with these not-so-healthy companies, but it's what the consumer does, needs, wants and desires that is important to sports. The connection with the consumer here is culture, leisure and recreation, including food habits, that are also significant. But letting these types of sponsors into a sport does come with a user-beware label and potential consequences, for example, viewers and spectators and fans getting caught in vices and addiction.

The move to health businesses and organizations in sport is seen as a natural link between them and sports. Many firms who are health-based have incorporated concepts and tools of commercial marketing into their sports sponsorship. The growth in health sponsorship came after the effects of and phasing out of tobacco advertising, for example with Motor Sports, which made sense because of the metaphors of fire and smoke, like how a motorcar functions, and the link with looking 'cool' with smoking and motorcars, and the Benson and Hedges International Cricket. There was also the health and fitness boom, which was an influence on people wanting to be healthy and having more knowledge and awareness of health, such as diet, exercise and gyms and therapy and stress management (Jalleh et al (Spring 2002)).

But what about the small-to-medium sized businesses who would like to sponsor sports? Some businesses think sports sponsorship is relegated to big business, who supposedly have the money and power to do so. This is far from the truth. A local business can sponsor a local sport, sporting team or athlete and gain a number of benefits, the same benefits a big company can gain. If the business wants to remain small and local with local sports sponsorship, then so be it, or become big and branch out, then that can happen to. There are plenty of sports and leisure activities around to sponsor. An owner or member of a local business might even have a son or daughter who plays for one of the local sporting teams and the business can sponsor such a team.

In stating this, sports sponsorship is growing more popular, and has been for a while now, but is still an important part of the marketing mix. The target market and consumer, and consumer behaviorr and evaluation of the sports sponsorship, need to be planned, included and established from the start to be effective. Furthermore, thinking long-term as well as short-term is important too, just like Coca-Cola did in maintaining its sponsorship of the 1996 and preceding Olympic Games. Health sports sponsorship, especially in a health and fitness era, is also on the increase and is important, whether the business is directly linked to health and sport or not, because health is a natural link to sport.

Bibliography

- Australian Sports Commission, 'Sponsorship' – About Us
  http://www.ausport.gov.au/about/sponsorships

- Grohs, Reinhard. Wagner, Udo. and Vsetecka, Sabine. (April 2004) Assessing the Effectiveness of Sport Sponsorships – An Empirical Examination, <u>Schmalenbach Business Review</u>, Vol. 56, pp. 119-138
  http://www.sbr-online.de/pdfarchive/einzelne_pdf/sbr_2004_april-119-138.pdf

- Jalleh, Geoffrey. Donovan, Robert, J. Giles-Corti Billie, and Holman, C D'Arcy J. (Spring 2002) Sponsorship: Impact on Brand Awareness and Brand Attitudes, <u>SMQ</u>, Vol. VIII, No. 1
  http://cbrcc.curtin.edu.au/reports_journal_articles/smq%208%2035-45.pdf

- Kim, Jin-Woo. 'The Worth of sport sponsorship: An event study', The University of Texas, Arlington, <u>Journal of Management and Marketing Research</u>
  http://www.aabri.com/manuscripts/09382.pdf

- Lobo, Antonio. Yayoi, Chester. Meyer, Denny (2007) 'The effectiveness of sports sponsorship in Australia: A study investigating the determinants of consumer buyer behaviour', <u>Faculty of Business and Enterprise: Swinburne University of Technology</u>
  http://researchbank.swinburne.edu.au/vital/access/manager/Repository/swin:11576

- Millward Brown (October 2006) 'Can Sponsorship be effective?'
  http://www.millwardbrown.com/Libraries/MB_Knowledge_Points_Downloads/MillwardBrown_KnowledgePoint_Sponsorship.sflb.ashx

- NSW Department of Sport and Recreation, 'Sponsorship' (About Sponsorship)
  http://www.dsr.nsw.gov.au/sportsclubs/ryc_sponsor.asp
- Personal Experiences:
  - I studied Sport Management and Communications (Journalism and Marketing) at a local university in Australia, and information on sponsorship in general was discussed.

Super sensitive $1 million retire

One million or two million

Some think one million is ample, others two million, but either way, one needs to tread carefully with their superannuation retirement.

Rose states how "Australians need more than $1 million in superannuation to fund a comfortable retirement." (August 3, 2015). For some, $1 million, let alone $2 million, is out of reach and they end up having around $500,000 instead. This shows how difficult it can be to amass $1 million or 2 million.

Rose continues by mentioning how "the average super payout at retirement is about '$160,000'… fewer than five people in every 1000 have a pooled super fund of $1 million. This shows how difficult it can be to amass $1 million or 2 million. Rose continues by mentioning how "the average super payout at retirement is about '$160,000'… fewer than five people in every 1000 have a pooled super fund of $1 million. (August 3, 2015)"

Australian Institute of Superannuation Trustees Chief Executive, Tom Garcia, states how the $1 million retirement fund is but a myth. Garcia states how $2 million is a more realistic figure.

Some get this threefold, from retirement superannuation, aged pension and personal savings. People can either save themselves, make own super contributions or come up with wealth creation ideas for their super or just plain wealth.

Industry Super Funds

Specific industry super funds tend to be more popular among super contributors and also give better returns for a given policy. A person might be in Retail, in Accounting or Trades jobs. These detailed industry super funds could well be the choice over general super funds. An example was Woolworths rewarding its staff with stock market shares from the company, which was considered a safe investment being a bricks and mortar company. According to Rose, "AustralianSuper is the country's largest managed fund with '$92 billion' (August 3, 2015).

Being Comfortable

Although the gap between rich and poor still remains, there is a growing middle class who 'want to live a comfortable life'. They are neither rich nor poor. They have kept money aside, including superannuation, to produce this comfortable lifestyle. If they need or want something, it is there, they can obtain it or little or no effort is required to get it.

Starting younger or older

Some people start saving from young, by having a career and or family from young. This means after their education, around 20-22 years of age, they start to work and earn money and put money aside for superannuation. This is a substantial amount of time in the workplace if the person continues to work until their 60's and retirement. Some have been in a number of jobs and workplaces with a variety of superannuation, most probably losing out to taxes and rates.

More people are starting young with personal savings the main income producer, as super and an aged pension years away. The thing is, and the way life expectancy is, some people die before reaching retirement and getting their hands on and use their superannuation. In my Dad's role as a Bus Driver, he saw many men die just before or a bit after retirement, not getting the chance to live a better life and enjoy their superannuation. Rose states that "in 40 years, a typical super payout would be worth about $500,000." (August 3, 2015).

Superannuation can be involved

To just rely on super can be tough and difficult, having to save 20, 30 or 40 years of hard work and effort showing in one's superannuation. People are beginning to show signs of wear in making their superannuation stretch up to and beyond retirement.

There are also plenty of get-rich-quick scams or funds producing poor results for an individuals superannuation. An example is the constant advertisements on the Internet marketing various wealth creation schemes. A better and wiser choice is researching various wealth creation ideas, strategies and projects, for example, a business, product or networking.

Era of Wealth Creation

There are good and bad get rich schemes around at the moment. Since a person cannot touch their superannuation until the age of 65 years and an aged pension for away, money either comes from personal savings or some form of wealth creation. This era could be classed, as the era of wealth creation. Some are afraid of it, as greed is not good, and some embrace it wholeheartedly becoming millionaires, even billionaires. There are products ideas with companies like Penny Miller, Innovations catalogue and Danoz Direct. There is networking with organisations like Network 21-Amway, GNLD and Isagenix and running a business idea or project, for example, finance, retail, food and drink and clothing.

Insurance companies

Obtaining Insurance is quite popular nowadays with a large number of insurance companies around. These companies provide Life Insurance, in case somebody dies or gets sick, Income Protection in case a person loses their job or gets sick, and Bill Relief if ever a person cannot pay a bill/s. Examples of Insurance are 'Insurance Line', 'Real Insurance' and 'Coles Insurance'. This could be in a way similar to wealth creation and a support to superannuation, especially the Life Insurance. From as little as $10-$30 a fortnight or month can see a person secure such insurance.

My Parents

My Father began his career in government Bus Driving late in the peace, having worked in retail clothing. He was in his mid-to-late 30's when he started Bus Driving. He had missed close to 20 years of producing superannuation from one or a few companies. My Father was a Bus Driver for 23-24 years. He became sick toward the end of his career due to stress reasons and he took sick leave. He had produced two years of sick leave, a few years before retiring. My father's brother-in-law was in consultancy and tried to urge my Dad to keep working, not understanding the state my Dad was in. After the sick leave, my Dad retired and got access to his superannuation.

Most of the superannuation went into paying off the mortgage of our house and investing in the house with some interior decorating, for example, cladding, timber floors and build in wardrobes. In 2014, my father's superannuation ran out. He wouild receive money from his pension, from money from his children living at home and also having to get a re-mortgage on the house despite having already paid it off.

Mortgage on a house and Everyday Living

Most people will not be able to get their hands on their superannuation until retirement. One of the biggest expenses for people, especially one-income and low income families or households is a mortgage or rent. More high income and double income families and households can pay off their mortgage sooner rather than later. My parents were one of the lucky ones to be able to have survived, staying together in marriage and eventually paid off the mortgage of the house with my Dad's superannuation.

Conclusion

For those who read this, start from young to amass a decent level of superannuation. Have a threefold level of income from personal savings and wealth creation, with superannuation and the aged pension later to follow. Making contributions to the superannuation fund will help create a proper amount to live upon in retirement, whether it be up to, or beyond $500,000 to a $1 million. Double or more income earners will always have the key to being financially stable, paying off a mortgage or investment, and having more money to give to superannuation.

Bibliography

- Rose, Sally. (August 3, 2015) 'MIlllon-Dollar super targets labelled scare campaign', Sydney Morning Herald